God's Gift For the Moment

God Will Never Take You to What
He Can't Bring You Through

KATHY BROADNAX

iUniverse, Inc.
New York   Bloomington

God's Gift For the Moment
God Will Never Take You to What He Can't Bring You Through

iUniverse books may be ordered through booksellers or by contacting:

iUniverse
1663 Liberty Drive
Bloomington, IN 47403
www.iuniverse.com
1-800-Authors (1-800-288-4677)

Because of the dynamic nature of the Internet, any Web addresses or links contained in this book may have changed since publication and may no longer be valid. The views expressed in this work are solely those of the author and do not necessarily reflect the views of the publisher, and the publisher hereby disclaims any responsibility for them.

ISBN: 978-1-4401-8214-3 (sc)
ISBN: 978-1-4401-8215-0 (ebook)

Printed in the United States of America

iUniverse rev. date: 8/20/2010

Contents

Part 1
First of All

First of all I would like to thank the Lord for the opportunity to share my gifts of writing poems with some of the world. My poems mean a lot to me because of the lost I've experienced in my life. And because of the lost of each person that has lost a loved one, or someone close to them. But by the grace of God, don't think of it as a lost; think of it as a cause, because God is greater than any lost

For The Moment

My book is a book of poetry in finding your way back,
to building a foundation for love, believing in your self,
courage, hope, fun, laughter, happiness, and a piece of mind,
give it to God as I did because God foundation is solid and
remember all poems are reversible

FOR THE MOMENT

For the moment has help me to deal with the lost of my beloved ones,
it has help me to express my feelings in dealing with depression.For the
moment has been a great inspiration in my life.

Part 2
About the Author

Part 2

I'm a wife and a mother of three daughter, one son, and eight grandchildren. Two grandsons and six granddaughter, I lost my son in a car accident, he was my one and only son. I felt my life was over, God what did I do wrong that you would take my child, my one and only son, my baby. Why God I cried so hard, my God this can't be true, God I loved him what did I do. I felt that my life was unworthy for I had betraded my son. His life was over at such a young age.I couldn't save my son. I wasn't there to say goodbye, people ask me if there was anything they could do for me, I would respond by saying if you can't give my son back then you can't help me. I wold lay awake at night wondering if my child was o.k, did he call for me and I wasn't their, So I ask God to show me how my son was doing. As he rock me to sleep I saw my son standing by a tree stump. The first thing I said to him was I love you son please come home. He look at me with a smile on his face, and said, I love you to mom, I'm happy mom. I'm happier than I have ever been, I wouldn't come back even if I had to. I said not even for me son not even for me, as I woke from my sleep I knew right then that my son was with God, but I didn't care I wanted my son to be here with me and his three sisters, he was happy here with me. I ask God why, why God am I being selfish and God respond by saying why why not you. There is a long rugged road that your son would have had to cross, you would not have been able to bare it, so as he have given his life I come to recieve it unto me, my son died with a smile on his face. I thought I was going to die when I saw my son lying there not able to move in his last home here on earth, but when I saw him and how peaceful he look. I smile and kissed my son for the last time. You never get over the lost of a love one no matter how hard *you try or how many years go by, and when a love one die they takes part of you with them. I struggled I looked for my son even though I saw my son body, I still didn't believe he was gone. I wanted to awake from this sleep because it was a nightmare. I lost twenty-eight pounds in just two weeks, I couldn't eat because the last thing you do is put your love one away, and the first thing you do is eat after it's over. I knew I had a husband, three daughters, and at the time four grandchildren, step children, sisters, and brothers to live for. I knew they love me but they couldn't help either, so I had to snap out of denier of losing my son, because he had peace with God and he was happy so I started focusing on my three year old daughter and my grandchildren. The more I focus on them the more the Lord help me to deal with the lost of my son. Even though it's been years there are times when I want to brake down but God lift me up and dry away my tears and let me know that because of the lost of my son, I can reach others thourgh writing poetry and let them know that there is a God. Try and focus on what we have left because there is nothing we can do about what we have lost but to pray and ask God to bless us that we may see them again someday.*

Part 3
You are my Rose Daughter

You Are My Rose Daughter

You are my rose
I asked for a flower
And God gave me a rose
What beautiful way to brighten my soul
The laughter, the joy
He sent my way
When he gave me this rose
On that special day
I will always be with you, but in your heart
Just like I was from the very start
So take my love and hold on tight
Because God love you and he knows what's right
You are my rose
I will never let go because I'm in your heart
And I love so

I Love My Son

Oh how sad it was that day when
God took my son away
My heart stopped on that day
The pain I felt wouldn't go away
I cried so hard, this can't be true
God I love him, what did I do
God please don't take him away
He is my baby, please let him stay
Now he's gone to a better home
I love my son, but I must move on

God having provided something better for us,
That they should not be made perfect apart from us.

Hebrews 11:40

My Darlin' Son

God heard him
Behold he came
Wiping away the tears
Taking away the pain
In heaven my child now he lay
Mom and dad will see you again someday
Now you are waiting with your crown
At home with Jesus
Your final round
We love you son
More than you will ever know
But God love you even more
Your work here has been run
Now you are free my darlin' son
So go head on and take your rest
God loves you and he knows what's best

To every thing there is season, and a time to every purpose
under the heaven:
A time to be born, and a time to die; a time to plant
and a time to pluck up that which is planted;
A time to kill, and a time to heal; a time to break down,
and a time to build up;

Ecclesiastes 3:1-3

You Will Be Missed My Darling Son

Now you are gone away from here
to a better home
Little did you know that God was there
with his arms wide open
to show he care
He had plans for you this special day
No one ,not no one could take them away
Mom loves you,Dad loves you too
But there is no greater love then what God has for you
We will see you son again some day
in that beautiful place where you lay
so go head on and take your rest
God loves you and he knows what's best
You will be missed my darling son
but your work here has been run

God having provided something better for us,
That they should not be made perfect apart from us.

Hebrews 11:40

In the Gates of Heaven

You are not forgotten
Nor are you gone to stay
You are just in a safe place
Until we meet someday
We miss you now more than you will ever know
But there is a great celebration
You and I both know
In the gates of heaven there where you wait
Until we meet someday
Beyond the heavenly gates

Preserved me. O God for in you I put my trust
O my soul, you have said to the Lord,
You are my Lord, my goodness is nothing
apart from you

Psalm 16:1-2

A Safe place

God saw you getting restless
And tired as can be
So he whispered
Come home and live with me
With painful heart I watch you
As you fade away
With all my love and prayers
I couldn't make you stay
And yet my heart was broken
When God took you away
He will keep you in a safe place
Until we meet again some day

And God will wipe away every tear from their eye;
There shall be no more deaths, nor sorrow, nor crying
there shall be nor more pain,
for the former things have passed away

Revelation 21:4

Little Did I Know

I was three when my brother died
Little did I know how much I cried
I will always remember his soft little hands
And how much he was a nice young man
He died with a smile on his face
Now he is in a safe place
He loved us with all his heart
Without him we fell apart
Now we are back together again
Because we know he's in a safe place
And he's watching us each and everyday

As he have heard
So we have seen
In the city of the Lord of host
In the city of our God
God will establish it forever

Psalm 48:8

Wasn't it you Grandma

Wasn't it you grandma who kept it real
Wasn't it you grandma who taught me not to steal
Wasn't it you grandma who told me not to fight
Wasn't it you grandma who stood up for what's right
Wasn't it you grandma who left me
Wasn't it you grandma who wanted your life to be free
Wasn't it you grandma who got the blessing
Listen I got only one more question
Wasn't it you?

Jquita Broadnax

Psalm 23

The Lord is my shepherd; I shall not want.
He makes me to lie down in green pastures:
he leads me beside the still waters.
He restores my soul; he leads me in the paths of righteousness
for his name's sake.
Yeah, though I walk through the valley of the shadow of death,
I will fear no
evil; for thou are with me; they rod and thy staff, they comfort me.
You prepare a table before me in the presence of my enemies;
thou anoint my
head with oil; my cup runs over.
Surely goodness and mercy shall follow me all the days of my life;
and I will
dwell in the house of the Lord forever.

Grandma Still Loves Us

My grandma is at rest
She did her very best
She lived her life for Christ
For yet he paid the price
Now grandma is gone on home
Her love will yet live on
She is gone to live with Jesus
In heaven, her new home
She knows she will see us
In heaven where she lay
There she will be waiting
Beyond that heavenly gate
Grandma still loves us
Don't cry, don't say good-by
Grandma will see us again
Beyond that great blue sky

I will love you, O Lord my strength
The Lord is my rock and my fortress and my deliverer
My God, my strength in whom I will trust
My shield and the horn of my salvation, my stronghold

Psalm 18:1-2

He Didn't See It Coming

He didnt see it coming
because it came so fast
when he closed his eyes
he was at home at last
sitting in his seat
across from Christ
with a smile on his face
that will forever last
he made it in
he was finally their
with angels all around
and love everywhere

Blessed is the man that walketh not in the counsel of the ungodly,
nor standeth
in the way of sinner, nor sitteth in the seat of the scornful.
But his delight is in the law of the Lord;
and in his law doth he meditate day and night.
And he shall be like a tree planted by the rivers of water
that bringeth forth his fruit in
his season; his leaf also shall not wither;
and whatsoever he doeth shall prosper.

Psalm 1:1-3

I Miss My Dad

When I go to sleep I think about my dad
When he died I felt so sad
I was only eleven months when he died
My mom told me that I cried
I felt so bad he was gone
I told God, I'm all alone
I'm my dad only child
That alone bring tears in my eyes
Dad was so young when he died
He had a smile on his face but yet I cried
Dad made peace with christ one day
At home in heaven now he lay
I knew some day I'll see my dad
and in his bulsom I will lay
I miss my dad every day
But I know God will make away

Demorrious Brown

Call upon me in the day of trouble I will deliver thee

Psalm 50:15

My Uncle Man

I was just a year old when my uncle died
But mommy told me that I cried
I don't remember my uncle face
But I bet it was as pretty as a red vase
My cosin Demorrious say he is all alone
Because my uncle is dead and now he is gone
But cousin you are not really all alone
Because you have family here at home
I know it's not the same as your dear young dad
But he want us to be happy and not be sad
So once again I want you to know
That you have family and I love you so

Kenneth Howard

God having provided something better for us,
That they should not be made perfect apart from us.

Hebrews 11:40

I Love My Uncle

Now my uncle is resting in peace
In heaven, is where his soul should be
Before he left, I song him a song
Because he was my uncle, my only one
Now he is gone, he truly will be missed
I love my uncle, to him a kiss

Jasmine Howard

In my father's house are many mansions;
If it were not so, I would have told you

John 14:2

God Grace

An Angel from heaven was sent your way
To tell his child to come home today
To deliver him from suffering and give him rest
Often he does this
Because he knows what's best
Now the time has come to take you home
So darling family don't worry, he is not alone
He ran his race, because God was their
He had Faith and courage
Did you know
God gave it to him because he love him so
He is in a better place, this we know
Because God grace tells us so
So don't worry, don't cry
don't say good-by
We will see him again beneath the sky

I love the Lord, because he has heard
my voice and my supplications

Psalms 116:1

In Memory of My Dear Mother

We love our dear mother
We miss her very much
That day when Jesus spoke
our hearts were really touched
Mother has gone on home
her love will yet live on
She has gone to live with Jesus
Don't cry, don't even moan
You see your mother is in peace now
no tears, not even pain
Mother is happy with Jesus
We will see her yet, again

reverse

To every thing there is season, and a time to every purpose
under the heaven:
A time to be born, and a time to die; a time to plant
and a time to pluck up that which is planted;
A time to kill, and a time to heal; a time to break down,
and a time to build up;

Ecclesiastes 3:1-3

In Memory of My Dear Father

We love our dear father
We miss him very much
That day when Jesus spoke
Our hearts were really touch
Father is gone on home
His love will yet live on
He is gone to live with Jesus
Don't cry don't even moan
You see father is in peace now
No tears not even pain
Father is happy with Jesus
We will see him yet again

Thou wilt shew me the path of life: in thy presence is fullness of joy; at thy right hand there are pleasures for evermore.

Psalm 16:11

My Grandma is at Rest

My grandma is at rest
for her love she gave best
Grandma lived a good and holy life
for she knew, that one day she would be with christ
As grandma lay with a smile on her face
At home with Jesus her brand new place
Grandma is happy and very content
For the life she live, where truly meant
So rejoice at the the things that grandma did
Because nothing she did, that she didn't repent
So dry those tears away from your eyes
And give God the glory, and Grandma a smile
Grandma will be seeing you again someday
At home with Jesus their she lay

To him who alone does great wonders, for his mercy endures forever

Psalm 136:4

When God Took Your Mom

When God took your mom away
He had a better place for her to stay
Your mom is gone to a better home
Don't worry son she is not alone
So don't cry or say good bye
Because your mom is beneath the great blue sky
You will see your mom again some special day
At home with Jesus where she lay

In my Father's house are many mansions: if I were not so, I would have told you. I
go to prepare a place for you.

John 14:2

True Angel of God

An angel of salvation was sent one rainy day
To tell a child of God the master is on his way
To deliver him from suffering and give him rest
Often did he realize his life was just a test
Now the time has come and my son has gone home
But family do not fret for he will not be alone,
He ran his race with faith and courage not once did my son quit
But never did he say good-bye, because good-byes do not exist
He is in a better place and truly will be missed
He's just a solider gone ahead he hasn't lost his way
He never said good-bye
Because he'll see you again someday

Sharon Brown

And God will wipe away every tear from their eye;
There shall be no more deaths, nor sorrow, nor crying
there shall be nor more pain,
for the former things have passed away

Revelation 21:4

Grandpa

Grandpa will be missed
But he is not gone to stay
He is gone to be with Jesus
In heaven where he lay
He said to us one day
His soul would be at rest
Don't cry when it happen
His life was just a test
So fell the joy and not the pain
For he is not far away
He is resting there in heaven
Until we meet someday

The earth is the Lord's and all its fullness the world
and those who dwell therein
For he has founded it upon the seas, and established it upon the water

Psalm 24:1-2

An Angel was Sent One Day

An angel was sent one day to tell his child that help was on his way
To tell him of salvation and how Christ rose one day
Never did he realize that his life would fade away

As he have heard
So we have seen
In the city of the Lord of host
In the city of our God
God will establish it forever

Psalm 48:8

God has the Final Say So

I know the love that you lost
I know the pain that it cause
I know the sorrow that it brings
I know the joy in between
I know that your mom is just a prayer away
I know that the only thing is, you can't see her everyday
I know that it seem that God wasn't there
and if he was he just didn't care
I know when the door is open it's time to go
I know that God does this because he loves us so
It's hard for us to understand, but if we did we would make better plans
No matter what pain it cause
God has the final say so for us all
So I'm saying this just for you
God loves you and I do too

To the Family

Don't fret
Don't cry
Don't say goodbye
Your brother is just beneath the sky
The pain he shared is gone away
What joy he has where he lay
The hurt, the tears he has no more
For God heard him and let him go
He knew his time was drawn near
By the pain he had when he was here
Now he is free this we know
Hold on to his love but let him go

all poems are reversible

As You Can See

My book is about me as you can see
My life my style as it used to be
The pain I shared, the tears I cried
The joy of rain drops falling outside
The gifts of love as you see
God great sunshine smiles on me
I am a mother of three daughters and one son you see
My son is gone on home to live with Jesus
here he use to be,
Here on earth with my three daughters and me
but time has changed since that day
The pain I shared has gone away
The hurt, the hunger for him to come home
Is gone, for he is not alone
He is there with Jesus as you see
Welcome home
Thank God he is free

Part 4
It's Difficult to Bare the Lost of a Love One and Many More

With Deepest Sympathy

It's diffcult to bare the loss of a love one
or some one so dear to you
When all we have left is memories of things that we use to do
We will keep the love and thoughts so very, very close
And the special memories to comfort our souls

With Sympathy in the Lost of a Love One

Love ones live in memory
The treasure of good times
The thoughts of happiness and wonders of all kinds
Even though they are gone in spite of all sorrow
The joy still lingers on in a bright and better tomorrow

God Loves You

May it be a source of comfort and inner strength to know
that God loves you and watching over you
through this time of need he'll stay close by your side
to ease your pain and sorrow and be your friend and guide

God Gates are Fill with Wonderful Flowers

God gates are fill with wonderful flowers
Some are still in full bloom
Some still are Rosebuds that maybe picked too soon
But God pick the perfect time together them around
And put them in a better place
In heaven where he is found
He looks through those flowers and picks the better one
And place them in a better place
With his begotten Son

God Cares for You

May it be a source of comfort
To know that God cares for you
At your time of sorrow
And through out your life time too

God Picks the very Best

God picks the very best in everythin he do and put them in a rose garden
Where everything is new and yet our hearts are filled with pain
Greed and sadness to
But God cares for us in all that he do

You Have My Deepest Sympathy

You have my deepest sympathy
I know what you are going through, because I've been there
It's so hard to bare right now, but times get better as the days go
By I can't say don't cry, don't weep. don't even moan
Because you love him and now he is gone
But remember God loves you and he's there both night and day
Just kneel down and begin to pray
He will make a way just wait and see
Because he made a way for my family and me
So you see I know that it seems that God wasn't there and if he
was he just didn't care
But he does, we know, he gave his son because he loves us so
It gets hard before it gets better, so do what yoou feel is good for
you because your son is gone
His work here is through, but remember he is just a prayer away
The only thing is you can't see him everyday
He loves you, and he always will
As you love him, he knows that still
He is still with you but in your heart
Just like he was from the very start
I love you with all my heart
My prayers are with you

Part 5
A Warrior Prayer
Hurricane Katrina
and Many More

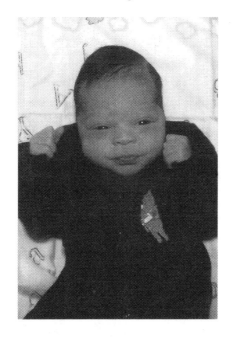

A Warrior Prayer

(Prayer Before Starting Your Day)

Heavenly Father, I bow down in worship and praise before you. Dear Lord, I cover myself with the blood of Jesus Christ and claim the protection of the blood for my family, my finances, my home, my spirit, my soul, and body. I surrender myself completely in every area of my life to you dear Lord. I take a stand against all the workings of the devil that would try to hinder me, and my family from best serving you. I address myself only to the true and living God, and refuse any involvement of Satan in my prayer. Satan, I command you and all your demon forces of darkness, in the name of Jesus Christ, to leave my presence. I bring the blood of Jesus Christ between the devil and my family, my home, my finances, my spirit, soul, and body, Lord, Jesus Christ. Furthermore, in my own life today, I destroy and tear down all the strongholds of Satan, and smash the plans of Satan that have been formed against my family and me. I tear down the strongholds of the devil against my mind, and I surrender my mine to you, blessed, Holy Spirit. I affirm, heavenly Father, that you have not given me the spirit of fear, but of power and love and of a sound mine (2 Timothy 1:7). Therefore, I resist the spirit of the enemy, and nothing shall by any means hurt me (Luke 10:19). I claim complete and absolute victory over the forces of darkness, in the name of Jesus and I bind the devil and command him to loose my peace, my joy, prosperity and every member of my family for the Glory of God, and by Faith, I consider it done. I break and smash the strongholds of Satan formed against my emotions today, and I give my emotions to You. I destroy the strongholds of Satan formed against my will today. I give my will to You, Heavenly Father, and choose to make the right decisions of faith. I breakdown the strongholds of Satan against my body today, and I give my body to You, realizing that I am the Temple of the Holy Ghost (I Cor. 3:16-17, I Cor. 6:19, 20). Again, I cover myself with the blood of the Lord Jesus Christ and pray that the Holy Ghost would bring all the work of the crucifixion, all the work of the resurrection, all work of the ascension of the Lord, Jesus Christ into my life today. I surrender my life and possessions to you. I refuse to fear, worry, or be discouraged in the name of Jesus. I will not hate, envy or show any type of bitterness toward my brothers, sisters or my enemies. But, I will love them with the love of God shed abroad in my heart by the Holy Ghost (Romans 5:5). Open my eyes and show me the areas of my life that do not please you and give me the strength, grace and wisdom to remove any sin or weight that would prevent our close fellowship. Work within me to cleanse me from all grounds that would give the devil a foothold against me. I claim in every way the victory of the cross over all satanic forces in my life. I pray in the name of the Lord, Jesus Christ with Thanksgiving and I welcome all the ministry of the Holy Spirit.

AMEN

Hurricane Katrina

Hurrican Katrina
Caught us by surprise
She took away lives
And brought tears in our eyes
So much sorrow, heartache and pain
Never did we realize how fast our lives could change
People are hollering from miles and miles away
Please help us, Dear Savior
Help us Lord we pray
But there were so many lost and lot's with no place to stay
There was some with homes and no lights to see their way
Darkness was up on them
Food was thrown away
Business was closed down
And not much gas to get around
People were in lines for hours at a time
Some were observing to see what others would do
Never did they realize that God was there too
Through all this heartache and pain
Bitterness and trouble too
This is just a wake up call
Time is drawing near
Take care of what you have left
And God will take care of you

The Lives She Took

The heat we have to bear
With no lights and no air
The children are frighten
Of the dark of night
With candle lights burning
And the fear of fright
Power is out all over town
With just a little hope of getting around
Oh what powerful and painful hurt
Of hurricane Katrina
And the lives she took
But we must move on and try to get ahead
Because there is nothing we can do
But pray instead
God loves us
He cares for us too
At times like this
What else can we do

My Heart Goes Out To You

My heart goes out to the families
Of the ones who lost there love ones
And their homes dew to hurricane Katrina
They truely are implaceable and really will be missed
But there is a reason for all things
And for all things there is a time
But we really must give it to God
And let him have his way just stay prayerful
Both night and everyday
God is good and great, we know
He does things that we don't understand
So we must be thankful in the things that he do
Because there is nothing, no nothing
That either one of us can do
So please try and be strong
And let God take care of you

Part 6
Slipping into a
Depressing Stage

God is with you

God is with you in your time of depression
Just hold on, don't let go
It seems like a long time
but it's sooner than you know
Time will come and change will take place
God will put peace in your heart
and a smile on your face
He love you more in your time of trouble
And your blessing he have will soon be double
So keep the faith
and hold on tight
Because God loves you and you will be all right

Depression

Depression is a time
When you really need to hold on to God
Because the devil will attack you
And break your heart
He will do all he can do
To take you down
And take your smile
And turn it upside down
So get on your knees
And begin to pray
Talk to God, he will make away

When You Find Yourself

When you find yourself thinking beyond your thoughts
Give it to God and he will work it out
There is power in God word
And more love then you have ever heard
God alone can see you through
Because he knows just what to do
So go head on give God a try
And don't let his love pass you by

Depress

Depressing is not of God love
But of the Devil and his world
So when your mind slip into another channel
Give it to God he knows how to handle
Your mind is a terrible thing to loose
So don't listen to the devil and his rules
Because his job is to take you out
And leaving you hanging without a doubt
But know that Jesus is able and he will work it out

Part 7
My Pets

Joe and Max

I have a pet his name is Joe
He is the sweetest pet I know
He has a friend, his name is Max
They are as close as cracker Jacks
Max is so fluffy, and as cute as can be
His eyes light up like a christmas tree
Joe is black with shiny hair
And takes off running, like a big black bear
But when he comes home, he plays with Max
And takes him for a ride upon his back

Kenneth Howard

Romeo

My dog name is Romeo
he runs and jumps
and plays with his toes
dance and sings
and eat onion rings
my dog can do most anything
he rides on the back of my goat
and laughs at me when I tell my jokes

Jalaha Howard

Bumble Bee

Bumble bee, bumble bee
don't sting me
take my apple
and let me be'
I'm not yours
please go away
don't come back
anymore today

Tomeal Howard

Natasha is my cat

Natasha is my cat
she is my favorite pet
when I go out and play
she gets right in my way
she loves for me to play with her
and rub her curly hair
kiss he on her nose
and call her teddy bear
she sleeps in my bed
right up above my head
and wakes me with her nose
nibbling on my toes

Jquita Howard

Part 8
A Family Reunion

Family Reunion

A family is more than a mom or dad, sister or brother
It's rejoicing and trusting in the Lord and being together with others
Being able to share the songs and dance a smile for stories untold
A family is full of memories to treasure as precious as gold
It's getting together and spreading cheer and lots of love too
It's taking the time for reuniting like families should often do
So take the time to say to them how much you miss them so
Because to someone you forgot, it's certainly good to know
From now on let's us keep in touch and not just once a year
There must be a special reason that God has brought us here
Together again with fun to share and new relatives to meet
We thank you Lord for reuniting us and we shall not forget
To keep in touch all year through as on our journey we go
Because someone is thought about more often than-u-know

Grandma

I have eight grandchildren
Six granddaughters and two grandsons
Each one of them loves bubble gum
And when they see me
They always say, I love you
Do you have any bubble gum today
And when they get it
They go out and play
And cone back in and say
How was you day
You are the best grandma
Everyone knows you are so sweet
And we love you so

God's Touch

God touch the heart of my grandchild
Who I love so very dear
She can't even walk or talk
But she spoke so very clear
Hallelujah, hallelujah
With her hands, upon her head
Her feet was pattering the floor
That child was not afraid
She gave God the glory
With hallelujah, hallelujah she said
She was in it so deep
When I call her she didn't hear
God had her doing the work
That you and I are suppose to do
If a baby can live for Jesus
Then how about you
Jesus don't care who he calls
Salvation is up to you
It's time to get right with Jesus
Because nothing else will do
You see my grandchild is only ten months
She was in her walker, that beautiful and glorious day
When God spoke to her, you know its time to pray
Death will sneak up on us, and it will be too late to pray
So get real with Jesus
That's all I have to say

Children from all Around

I know some how and some way we are going to make it
In this world today with so much sunshine
And love of all kind, children from all around
In every city and every town
The joy that they have will truly keep us around

All the Boys and Girls

Children are so special
They are so sweet and kind
They have a way of loving you
and yet blow you mind
The things they do and say
are so amazing too
there kind and tender touch
Means so much to you
I love all little children
They will someday rule the world
They are a gift to us from God
All the boys and girls

My Sister in the Minstery of Music

My dear sister in the minstery of music
and in each word she know how to use it
The songs we sing is like we dreaming
in every word there is true meaning
We sing for Christ from the bottoms of our hearts
and every word tare us apart
The saints are falling all over the place
for truely God had made away
The choir was down too
For I knew right then
God was not through

From The Street's of Drugs To My Brother In Christ

I have a brother his name is Bell
and behind his name there is a story to tell
From the street's of drugs to the walk's of God
and how one day God saved his soul
God brought him from darkness into the marbles light
and every since then his soul have been right
At one time life didn't matter the devil was in control
of this dear fellow
The drugs he did, the games he played
had no meaning of the price christ paid
But then one day God stretched out his arms
and said come on in my darling son
And on that day he put drugs away
for he new right then that God had made away

Smell the Roses

You see now just yourself
because your love is all you have left
and when you dream, it's all about you
because no one else would ever do
so wake up from out your sleep
and smell the roses, they are so sweet

Tomeka Howard

God Gave us Children

God gave us children
To brighten our lives
They are like flowers
They need to be treated really nice
Teaching of the word
And the love of Christ
And the whip he took
To better our lives
And how he died
Hanging on the cross
And rose again
Because he loves us so

My Family

My family is special
They are also sweet
They are the kings of family
You would love to meet
They are gentle and kind
With open mind
They will be there for you
Through your worst of times
Because they care
They will be right there
Through the sun or rain
Just call our their name

Sister

With a sister like you
Someone who cares
God goodness and grace
Will always be there
He shines upon you
Like a morning star
Because he cares for you
Wherever you are
The joy, the love
The spirit you have will always be with me
Because I know you care

My Brother

I love my brother
With all my heart an soul
No matter what I do
He keeps me in control
He stands by my side
Each and everyday
He cares for me
I know he loves me too

Part 9
Rain is Pouring Down

Rain is Pouring Down

Rain is pouring down on the dirty streets
While crack heads is on the side of them asking the Lord
"WHY ME"
and its dark outside and they are saying to themselves
only if I did right
I will be inside a house where there is light
But it's not to late for them to leave that stuff alone
And start a new life inside a home
They need to do it, while its not too late
Because some people go to sleep and don't awake the only
person that got them doing is Satan
So they need to stop and open their eyes and realize them
Compromise
That there is still time to clean themselves up and their
mind
And move on up the road and tell Satan he can't have
your soul
It belongs to God and that's where it's going to stay
Because God is going to bless you each and everyday

Jquita Broadnax

God will take care of you

God will take care of you
Even though you are bad and good
He cares for you
What ever you do
Because he is God
And he loves you

Katherine Howard

The Grass is Green

The grass is green
The sky is blue
Jesus love you and me
The flowers are colorful
The tree trunk is brown
Jesus is the king who wears the crown
The house is beautiful
The sun is yellow
Jesus is a handsome young fellow
Airplanes fly across the beautiful sky
While babies are waving their hands saying good-bye

Jquita Broadnax

Great Times

There are places that you can go, and have great times
that will always be on your mind
you don't even have to go anywhere
because you can dream
when you are dreaming in real life
to you that's how it seems
you can just sit down and think
while you think you can drop down
writing with ink
you can sit down
and think about great times because the great
times won't go anywhere
it will still be on your mind

Jquita Broadnax

J. J. N. O. J.
In The Name Of Jesus

I look into your eyes and what a wonderful sight
A vision of Jesus in the middle of the night
I turn my head to see if it was true
Was it really Jesus or was it just you

Then an angel appeared with a sigh that read
In the name of Jesus above my head
Then I thought to myself my pastor is true
He calls on Jesus in what ever he do

Even before service my pastor would say
In the name of Jesus and begim to pray
So before I start my new day
In the name of Jesus is what I will say

So thank you pastor
For these encouraging words
They are better then any words
That I've ever heard

Bad Times

Everybody have bad times
that you can't get off your mind
so you need to drop down
turn around face the bad
and bow your head
pray to God as much as you want to
because no body can't stop you
just because you pray don't mean you're wrong
your prayers can be short
or they could be long
you can pray at the store
or at your home
you can pray anywhere and everywhere
you can pray here or there

Jquita Broadnax

The Heaven Above

The heaven above is somewhere, where there is nothing but
love
The streets are made of gold, and up there is nothing but good
souls
Up there you should wear a crown
because when you're down on earth you did good the first
time around
up there, there are no drugs and nobody trying to be bad
up there it's nothing but good thangs
unlike on earth it's violence
but in heaven it's not violence
tell every one don't keep it silent

Jquita Broadnax

Lord I Really Thank You

Lord I really thank you for this blessed day
For your son, Jesus
And all that he does
For the sun and rain
The joy and the pain
The hope and the sorrow
Thank you for your love
Because we know without your love
We couldn't love
Thank you for being you

He Died for Our Sins

The grass is green
The sky is blue
The Lord looks down
And smile on you
The street is bumpy
The grass is smooth
God will never make
A mark out of me or you
He died for our sins
For every last human being
That's why he can forgive us
and we must believe him
and always have trust
They put God on the cross
and did a sacrifice
That's why you should believe
in Christ

Jquita Broadnax

One Painful Day

When someone you love goes away
Go down on your knees
And begin to pray
Talk to God
He will make away
Just as he die for me
One painful day

God has Open the Gate

When you're here and thinking you're going to hell
Get down on your knees and say devil you're a tell
When you go to heaven, you will see gold
You will leave your bones and take your soul
Down on earth God has touched your hand
And said it's time for you to jump for joy and dance
God has open the gate
So you can go to heaven away from Satan
You can stay out of trouble
So all the things you did won't double
Up there you will see some of your friends
That's when you can say I'll be your friend to the end
Up there you can smile
But while you're up there you will still be looking down
While we're looking up
Saying now you're dead that really sucks
But we know what's best
So go ahead and take your rest

Jquita Broadnax

I Love You Lord

I love you Lord for what you've done
You sent your son Jesus, your only son
To prepare a place for the old and young
Up in heaven with your darling son
So thank you Lord for all you're done
You sent your only, begotten son

Sometimes

Sometimes we say things that we really don't mean
When we know within our hearts we must repent
We hurt, we cry, we sometimes moan
But in this world we're not alone
So please forgive us Lord today
Because life is to short to play this way
So as we go from day to day
Hear me Lord as I pray

Talk to God about Everything

When you are sad, don't get mad get glad
Get on your knees and start praying
Talk to God about anything or everything
So he can fix things and make it right
He will make you feel so good inside
That everything bad will just fade away

Jquita Broadnax

Jesus Died

Jesus died on Calvary
So that your soul and my soul
will someday be free
The sin that we cause
our soul was not loss
He took it all away one day
Hanging on the cross
To show us that he loves us
He died for us all

Give it to God

When it is time to go home toGod
You will be miss, from the very start
Your love one's is in and out of your life
But give it to God , he paid the price
We have our up's we have our downs
But God has the final round
We will have our teary moments
But God has our finally moments
So give it to God, what ever you do
Because God will take care of you

Katherine Howard

Thank You for this Day

Dear, O precious God
Thank you for this day
Another day that I've never seen
and you bless me anyway
You bless my loving children
as they went out to play
you bless them to come back in
allowing them a chance to pray
you bless me with a job
though sometimes it gets hard
But with your grace and love
It's not tearing me apart

May Peace be with you

*May peace be with you, in what you do
Kind and goodness be there too
Love and joy in all you do
God got his angels watching over you*

God Got the Victory

I read my bible everyday
I talk to God as I kneel and pray
Move Satan, stay out my way
God got the victory here today

You are My Everything

You are my everything
You are my love
My life
My joy, when there is sorrow
My hope, for tomorrow
My pick me up, when I'm down
My laughter, when I'm sad
My healer, when I'm hurting
My prayer mate, when I'm praying
My listener, when I'm talking
My speaker, when I'm silent
My soul mate at all times
My gentle touch, when I'm touching
My light, in the dark
My pathway, when I'm crossing
My teardrop, when I'm crying
My healer at all times
My food, when I'm hungry
My water, when I'm thirsty
You are my everything

God Can Hear You

God can be very silent
he can hear you
When you are violent
he knows just what you are going to do
That's when he steps in and takes care of you
So be careful with what you do or say
Because God can hear you everyday

Give God a Try

You should learn to depend on God
Go on it's not hard
And when you do
He will take care of you
Because that's his job
What else can he do
God is good
You and I both know
He gave his son
Because he loves us so
So go head on
Give God a try
He will take care of you
If only you try

Part 10
For a Wonderful Mom and Many More

For a Wonderful Mom

I thank you mom
For the love you have for me
For the sacrifice you made for me
For the understanding you showed me
For the many things you do for me
Now that I'm all grown up
I understand what a loving a mom you are to me
And I'm so very thankful to have a wonderful mom
Like you

Happy Mother's Day

My Mother worked her Fingers

Dear Oh precious God
Hear me yet I pray
Help my precious people
Throughout this blessed day
Help us to be with each other
And never ever depart
To show my dear oh mother
We love her very hard
My mother worked her fingers
And hurt them to the bone
To show us that she loves us
And gave us all she owned

Great Advice

Mom you have lots of faith and courage
You inspire my soul with what you know
You have given me great advice and saved my life
Not once but twice
I know I can count on you and what you say
Because you are my mom and you pray
Both night and day

Mom I Know

Mom I know this day
Maybe a very difficult day
For you
But stop and look around and know
That the Lord is always here for you
And so am I
I love you, mom

Latasha Howard

Mother's Day Wish

The most kind of mother's day wish
Is love, caring and lots of kisses
Hugs, smiles and sharing too
Because you are mother
And we care for you
We love you, mom

Happy Mother's Day

My Mother is like a Flower

My mother is like a flower
Her love grows and grows
Her love is going down in a row
She stand long and tall
Her love is greater than all
She stands up so strong
All her children are beside her
So she's not alone
She loves to shine
Like a diamond ring
Her joy is like a bell ringing

Wishing You Mom

Wishing you mom, with lots of love
All the sunshine
Joy and laughter, to brighten your days
And if only you knew how much I do love you
Mom do you know there's so much
That I want to say but can't
Any way, I do: I do love you

Latasha Howard

Mom I Love You

Mom I love you, just for being you
Not for the things you do for me
Not for nourishing me, when I'm sick
Not for feeding me, when I'm hungry
Not for giving me water, when I'm thirsty
Not for clothing me, when I'm naked
Not for my falling down and my getting up
Not for prayers, when you pray for me
Not for good times or the bad times
Not for the crying, when I'm sad
Not for the trouble, that I cause
But because you are the greatest mom of all
I love you
I love you
I love you mom

Happy Mother's Day

Mom my lope for you

Mom my love for you
Is like a leaf that falls
From a tree above
Without you I wouldn't be here
Because you brought me in this world
And because of that I'm grateful for you
And everything you do
So know that it's true
That I do love you

Happy Mother's Day

Latasha Howard

We both Love you

Faith and courage and good luck too
Is what I have, when I'm with you
So take your time and say good night
Don't worry about the bed bugs
They can't bite
Mom and dad is here just for you
We both love you
God do too

Our Very Special Mother

*Today is special
because its for you
Our very special mother
and all she do
We love you mother
just for being you
And we want to thank God
for giving us you*

A Mother's Love

Mother's are very special
because of the things they do
keeping the house together
and taking care of you

Other things they do
to brighten up your life
teaching you about christ
and how he paid the price

How they use their finger's
and work them to the bone
to show you that they love you
and give you all they own

Each time I look at mother
and all the things she do
there is no greater love
then what mother's have for you
so

Recieve your mother with love
and lots of kisses too
because there is nothing in this world
that mother won't do for you

When I First Meet You

When I first meet you, I knew you was meant for me
they always say the best things in life comes free
I never meet anyone as amazing as you
Lets do the math you and me equals two
A couple that's going to last
Until the day come to past
When the good Lord call us home
But until then your not alone
We both know God doesn't make mistakes
He knew what he was doing when he sent you my way

Happy Mother's Day

Pinkie Howard

Sweetheart

Sweetheart
you will always be
the most important part of my life
You are my dream come true
You are the apple of my eye
My heart belongs to you

Happy Mother's Day

Part 11
Celebrity's

Montel Williams and Oprah Winfrey

Montel and Oprah
Are somewhat the same
They cry, they mourn
Because they fell your pain
Then they do what's best
For you in getting you help
To see you through
What great love that God has given
To make your life be worth living

Dr. Martin Luther King

Dr. Martin Luther King was great you know
He change this world, because he love us so
The life he lived, the walk he took
Made history now it's in a book
He dream one day that we all would be free
Look at your brother, now look at me
Life has change as you can see
Thank God for Dr. Martin Luther King
and his Dr.'s degree

Michael Jackson

Michael Jackson was on a palace scope
He had lots of friends he had lots of hope
Then justice came and took them away
Leaving him with no place to stay
The price he paid for one mistake
Took his life, and throw it away
He has children of his own
What makes you thing
He would do others wrong
It was the public that put him on top
Now it the public that wants him stopped
But if he did wrong, they would have taken
his children away
because the law we have don't play that way
Children's life's are more important than money
Don't play that way, because that's not funny
His children has to grow up someday
And hear this talk about their dad
will turn them away
We love our children, don't teach them wrong
Give them good advice and keep them home
No child should have to live this way
Because there is already to much wrong in this world today
So think about the children in what you say
And how this will affect them along the way
I don't care how rich or famous you may be
When it comes to children life that's history
So get off your horse and throw away the rope
Don't play with children
Their life is no joke

A Dream

Martin Luther King went to sleep
and had a dream
That one day the world will change
That people like you and I
one day will be free
That whites and blacks will be able to talk
Not only can they talk but they can also walk
side by side with each other
That blacks won't have to be slaves
and they can spend time with their family
That you won't have to hurt your back
that all people can drink from a water fountain
they can get together and climb a mountain
we all can have fun, because our freedom is won

Jquita Broadnax

Oprah Winfrey

Oprah Winfrey reached her goal
She is a beautiful woman
with a wonderful soal
It took sometime
for her to get this way
After all Rome wasn't built in just one day
I adore her in the things she do
It brings out the best
and good in you
She works really hard to prove to you
that she does her best in what she do
She is really good, great and kind
and love by many and all man kind
So go ahead Oprah
Here's to you
God bless America and God bless you

Part 12
From Heaven Above
A Marriage Recipe
and Many More

From Heaven Above

You are sweet as candy
more lovely than gold
with beautiful words
to comfort my soul

A morning star
that shine so bright
and you touch my heart
in the middle of the night

You came into my life
with lots of love
even with the angels
from heaven above

Candy is sweet
and tasty to
but there is no candy
as sweet as you

A Marriage Recipe

1 Woman
1 Man equal to two cups of yoke
2 Cups of tender loving care, meaning that's no joke
3 Cups of faith, courage and understanding
because in a marriage that's demanding
4 Cups of trust and humility
because that's your responsibility
5 Cups of dependability
because that's what it use to be
Mix it together with lots of prayer
because God will answer
He will be right there
Add a lot of reassurance
because God knows what he is doing
6 Lbs. Of honest
because that's what God wants it be
Simmer your recipe and take your time
because true love in a marriage is hard to find
So keep prayer in this recipe
Because tender loving care is what it's meant to be

Dearly Beloved

Dear beloved the time has come
When you join hands together, you become one
Your love , your thoughts, your dreams come true
Because God is with you, in everything you do
There will be times when trouble appears
But remember God, because he is always here
God loves you daughter
He loves you son too
That's why he put you together
No one else could do
God knows our heart, he knows our mind too
Another reason he put you together
To become one not two

A Wedding Wish

May you find peace and joy
in everything you do
To celebrate your love
through out your life time to

Part 13
The Love of my Life
and Many More

The Love of my Life

I left my home in Georgia
Following the love of my life
He treated me with passion
And ask me to be his wife
Now our love is greater than it was before
He is the love of my life
And now I'm his wife

I've been in Love Before

I've been in love before
And its let me down
Now I am all grown up
And you are not around
Its time to pick up the pieces
Once again
Now I'm in love with someone else
And it's never been better
Better then any love I've ever known

Latasha Howard

Honey I love you

Today and always dear
My heart goes out to you
No one, not anyone
Could take the place of you
Because I think so much of you
On this special day
I would like to take the time
To say

Happy Valentine's Day

My love for you

My love for you
My love for you is like a dream come true
Without you boy what would I do
With the love that I have for you
And know matter what
My love for you will always be true

Latasha Howard

True Love

True love: true love is hard to fine
True love will blow your mind
True love please take your time
Time to shine and fine the one to wine and dine
Truelove is when two people combine
So take you time and fine a true love like mine

Latasha Howard

No Matter What they Say

No matter what they say
I will never leave you for anyone
No matter what they say
My love for you is greater
Than it's ever been
No matter what they say
I will always love you
And I will be there for you

Latasha Howard

Why Love

Why: Why love when you hurt so bad
Cry: Why cry when crying only makes you sad
Its bad to say that love can make you feel that way
But why love
When the one that you love so much
Makes you not trust that special touch
So why love, why love at all

Latasha Howard

You are so very special

You are so very special to me
I love you in every way
I can't imagine my life without you
My world wouldn't be the same
Every sound and tear drop
Would cause me so much pain
So darling here's to you
My love will always be true

No Matter What

No matter what they say
I will never leave you for anyone
No matter what they say
My love for you is greater than it's ever been
No matter what they say
I will always love you
And I will be there for you
When ever you need me

Latasha Howard

What Happen to the Boy

What happen to the boy I use to know
What happen to the boy I use to love
What happen to the boy you use to be
What happen to my baby... ... ...
Can somebody tell me
Where did he go, I miss my baby
Where did I go wrong
What mistake did I make

Latasha Howard

This Love we Share

This love we share
Is an everlasting love
So love me the way I want to be love
This love we share means so much
Your tender touch, I want so much
I want to know if this love we share will
Forever be

Latasha Howard

What is Love

Love is what you make of it
Love is spending time
Love is being around until
the test of time
When two people love each other
nothing can stop
there mind those two hearts
that beat together
will soon beat as one

Pinkie Howard

When you are not around

When I was visiting you in town
It was you that I found
I know my love was meant to be true
Because all I do is dream of you
And when you are not around
It seems my life is upside down
Now baby I'm here in town with you
Because no one else would ever do

Your Love

Your love is like a work of art
Design to fill the empty spot
For all the world to know
The wonder of your love
And the action that is shown

Since you like to play with Fire

You're a cheater and a liar
Since you like to play with fire
Then I'm going to let it burn
Last time was the last time
So I'm through with you
Your chance is over
When you had me you acted undercover
You tried to make me suffer
But since you been gone
I got tougher

Now We are Through

Now that I'm all alone
My love for you is finally gone
You left me one sunny day
You broke my heart
When you went away
You left the children
You hurt them too
But now they are finally over you
What we had
I thought was true
But you left me
an
Now we are through

My Love

My love, my dream really did come true
In all my dreams, I'm dreaming of you
Your eyes, your hair, your beautiful look
Stole my heart, that's all it took

There are so many things

There are so many things that I love about you
The way you smile in all you do
Your touch, your laugh, the color of your hair
In all you do, to prove you care

Part 14
*Birthday Wishes
and Many More*

Happy Birthday Friend

May each day begin and end
With wonderful thoughts of you being my friend
In case this break you down
Here is my towel, to pick you up
And bring you around

Happy Birthday

May your Birthday Wish Come True

God bless the wonders of your heart
Because he loves you from the start
So may your birthday wish come true?
In all the blessing
God have for you

Happy Birthday

Birthday Wish

Hope your birthday wish comes true
As mines did when I wish for you

Happy Birthday

Happy Birthday

Happy birthday to you
You are not one
Not two, not three
You see
But now four
And as beautiful
As can be

Happy Birthday

Happy Birthday

Here's to you
Lots of hugs and kisses too
And the many gifts we have for you
To make your birthday dreams come true

Happy Birthday

Happy Birthday to my Wife

Love is caring in everyway
Love is sharing day to day
Love is giving from the heart
Love is being there from the start
Love is what I have for you
You are my wife and I love you

Happy Birthday

Happy Birthday

To a wonderful friend
It's a special day
For wishing you the
Desires of your heart
And saying a friend
Like you just gets
Nicer as the years go by

A Wonderful Friend

I'm thinking of all the days
In my life
I spent not having you around
Wearing a smile on my face
Turned upside down
Now I'm thinking of the wonderful
difference it makes having you here
wearing a smile on my face
from ear to ear

For a Wonderful Friend

We've been friends for such a long, long time
We can't just stop, that would blow my mind
True friends are so hard to find
I would like to thank you
For being a friend of mines
Thank you friend
For such wonderful times
And for being so kind and a loving friend of mines

Thank you for being so dear to me

Our friendship is not hard to see
You were there when I needed you
Our friendship is not due
You always kept it real
You made me feel the way I suppose to feel
When I had some teardrops
You were there to tell me to stop
Now we can be friends
To the end

Jquita Broadnax

Thank You for your Support

Just writing to say how much I appreciate you
for the love, support and effort
and that included everything you have done for my family
and me
Just so you will know, we all are pleased and thankful too
Really just to have such a person as wonderful as you
You are young and very bright, not only in your heart
but in Jesus Christ, that's what makes you so special
Dear one we admire you so very much
Being young and intelligent with lots of patience too
And you always show gratitude in everything you do
That's very rare for young people today
But I thank God for sending you our way
Keep the good work up
And hold on to your patience, because we all know that
God has plenty of blessings for you in store one day

Part 15
What's Missing and Much More

What's Missing

One day I asked God
What was missing from my life
I felt complete, but my soul weeped
I felt I had the love, yet it wasn't from above
I felt I had friends who would be with me unto
the end
I felt I had joy, confidence and assurance
I felt I had experienced pain
I felt I had been through the rain
Yet there was something missing
this made me feel strange
I felt I had already been criticized
if not I apologize
Now I realize it was God who was missing
from my life
Thank you Lord for insight and your assurance
wrapped up with endurance

Sharon Brown

The Words close to My Heart

The Lord is my Shepard
I was told
and every since I read the word
I was sold
Now I hold the 23 Psalm
Close to my heart
and the words and I
will never part

Sharon Brown

I Need the Quiet

I needed the quiet
Not enemies, fast lanes
And someday life in prison
But a beautiful valley
of blessing instead
A place to grow richer in Jesus
Yes the only place to hide
I needed the quiet
So he drew me aside
Now you only have sweet memories
You hold inside
I needed the quiet
So he gently laid me aside

Sharon Brown

Church Mother

God is so merciful that he gave us a mother to teach and guide us in
loving
one another
A bond that is so special much stronger than glue, as unique as you are
there's only one you
You are the Church mother that bonds us forever to teach us to go on in
any
kind of weather
So gracious everlasting and so sincere too, no one will ever take the place
of
dear you
We all are rejoicing that you are here, once again to celebrate years past
and to be present with relatives and friends
May God forever bless you
Our dear Church mother

Sharon Brown

Neighbors

It was an honor to have neighbors like you
Kind, thoughtful and wonderful too
Loving and caring in all you do
There are so many wonderful things about you
You will be missed in this part of town
But the love you shared will still be around

Happy Father's Day

It's amazing to have someone like you
To share warmth and happiness in everything you do
You are so special, kind and sweet
And peaceful as can be
Beautiful and perfect and very important to me
Happy Father's Day
Dad

I Love You Sweetheart

All my love for you, on this special day
May it be the kind of love that nothing can take away
I love you sweetheart

Happy Valentine's Day

My Husband

He is a very special part of me
As loving as a man can be
He is everything in my life
He is always there to see me through
and make my life feel brand new
No one else could ever do
You are my husband
I love you

Happy Father's Day

Dad When I was a Child

You were there for me
You listen to me, when I talked
You helped me, when I learn to walk
You read to me, when I didn't know how
You were there for me, when I went to school
You helped me with my schoolwork
You took me to my class
You played with me, when I was lonely
You bandaged me, when I had a cut
You kissed me, when I cried
You hurt when I was hurting
You kneel on your knees, when we prayed
You said good night to me with a smile on your face
As you turn out the lights, you said good night, again
Dad you are the apple of my eye
I love you still

Happy Father's Day

Part 16
Season's Greetings

Fall

Fall is a season that comes and goes
With the beautiful leaves
Falling down in a row
You can see the leaves fall from miles
The color is so beautiful
It makes you smile
The shape of a leaf is so pretty to me
Because it's shaped like a
Christmas tree

Merry Christmas

The weather is cold outside
But my heart is warm
Because of the love and joy
That Christmas brings
And happy thoughts of everything

Merry Christmas

May Gods love
Smile on you doing Christmas
And throughout the New Year too
Merry Christmas

Merry Christmas

Thinking of you and wishing you
Health and happiness
Throughout the New Year
Have a bless and happy holiday season

Jingle Bells

Jingle bells are ringing
Toys Santa is bringing
Joy to the world for all the boys and girls
Merry Christmas to you
And a Happy New Year too

Christmas Day

Christmas day is finally here
Twelve whole months and a lot
Of good cheer
Merry Christmas to all
And to all a Happy New Year

Christ was born on Christmas Day

Away in a manger Christ lay in the hay
What a glorious and wonderful day
He came, our Savior this glorious day
Merry Christmas to all and have a
Happy holiday season, too

Merry Christmas

Merry Christmas
Glorious to God
This blessed day
Away in the manger the Savior lay
Happy holiday season
Thank God today
Joy to the world
This Christmas Day
Have a bless and wonderful New Year

Wishing you Every Reason

Wishing you every reason for the joy
Of the holiday season
And throughout the New Year
Merry Christmas

May your Christmas

May your Christmas and New Year bring
Joy to the world and a lot of good things
Merry Christmas
And a bless New Year

God's Angels

May peace be with you, in what you do
Kind and goodness, be there too
Love and joy in all you do
God has his Angels watching over you
Have a happy holiday season
And a bless New Year
Merry Christmas

May this Christmas

May this Christmas bring a blessing to you
With joy to the world and a Happy New Year, too
Merry Christmas

May your Home be filled with Lots of Love

May your home be filled with lots of love
And happiness too
May God bless you in all you do
Merry Christmas and Happy New Year, too

Merry Christmas

Behold he has come, Christ Jesus
The begotten son
Christ was born on Christmas Day
Away in a manger
My Savior lay
Have a bless Christmas
And
A Happy New Year

May your Christmas

May your Christmas be blessed and filled
With love and happiness, joy and lots of good cheer
Have a bless Christmas and a Happy New Year, too

May the Joy of Christmas

May the joy of Christmas come your way
With hope of happiness and toys to play
Merry Christmas to you
And
A Happy New Year too

Wishing you lots of Love

Wishing you lots of love on this Christmas Day
With all Gods blessing coming your way
Joy and happiness, good health too
And all the wonderful things
Christ has for you
Merry Christmas
And
A Happy New Year too

Christmas Day is Finally Here

Christmas day is finally here
O what joy Christmas brings
To everyone it's not a dream
To open a toy that Santa brings
Christmas Day is finally here
Joy to the world and lots of good cheer

Christmas Day

Christmas is a blessing to us
Because of Christ Jesus
In God we trust
The loving things you have given this day
Peace and happiness and a time to pray
A lot of good food and toys to play
Joy to the world
Thank god we pray
For the wonderful things
On this Christmas Day

Warm Wishes

Warm wishes to each one of you
Merry Christmas to all
And
A Happy New Year too

Happy Holiday Season

*May the best of the season
Bring you peace and happiness
For that reason
Have a bless holiday and a Merry Christmas*

Merry christmas

*Here's wishing that
a wonderful holiday reason
bring you happiness
for the wonderful holiday season*

Happy Holidays, God Bless America

Happy holidays, God bless America
And God bless you
Merry Christmas to all
And a Happy New Year too

Happy Holidays

May your every thought come true
And all the joy due to you
And your wish of Christmas cheer
Bring the best throughout the
New Year
Merry Christmas

Merry Christmas

Joy to the world
All the boys and girls
Joy to Christ on Christmas day
Joy to you and me
Be bless on Christmas day
And throughout the New Year too

Merry Christmas

Wishing that your home be filled with love
And your Christmas be filled with cheer
Throughout Christmas and the coming New Year

Merry Christmas

Grace and mercy
God has given
Joy to the world and lots of good living
Happy New Year
The whole year through and all your love ones
God bless you

Merry Christmas

Sympathy Cards
And
Greeting Cards
of your Choice

Get your needs meet call
Or
visit me @ www.kathybroadnax@yahoo.com
all cards are reversible

For the Moment

By: Kathy Broadnax
&
Glorfied works